創意，從無到有

A Technique
for
Producing Ideas

A Technique
for
Producing Ideas

經營管理 121

創意，從無到有
（原書名：創意的生成）

A Technique for Producing Ideas

Original English language edition copyright © 2003 by The McGraw-Hill Companies, Inc. through the Chinese Connection Agency, a division of the Yao Enterprises, LLC.

Chinese (complex character only) translation copyright © 2009 by EcoTrend Publications, a division of Cité Publishing Ltd. All rights reserved.

作　者：楊傑美　James Webb Young
譯　者：許晉福
封面 ‧ 版型 ‧ 插圖：廖韡 Liaoweigraphic
責任編輯：林昀彤
行銷業務：劉順眾、顏宏紋、李君宜
總 編 輯：林博華
發 行 人：凃玉雲
出　版：經濟新潮社
104 台北市民生東路二段 141 號 5 樓｜電話：(02)2500-7696｜傳真：(02)2500-1955
經濟新潮社部落格：http://ecocite.pixnet.net

發行：英屬蓋曼群島商家庭傳媒股份有限公司城邦分公司｜台北市中山區民生東路二段 141 號 2 樓｜客服服務專線：02-25007718；25007719｜24 小時傳真專線：02-25001990；25001991｜服務時間：週一至週五上午 09:30-12:00；下午 13:30-17:00｜劃撥帳號：19863813；戶名：書虫股份有限公司｜讀者服務信箱：service@readingclub.com.tw｜香港發行所：城邦（香港）出版集團有限公司｜香港灣仔駱克道 193 號東超商業中心 1 樓｜電話：852-25086231｜傳真：852-25789337｜E-mail: hkcite@biznetvigator.com｜馬新發行所：城邦（馬新）出版集團 Cite (M) Sdn Bhd 41, Jalan Radin Anum, Bandar Baru Sri Petaling,57000 Kuala Lumpur, Malaysia.｜電話：(603) 90578822｜傳真：(603) 90576622｜E-mail: cite@cite.com.my

印刷 宏玖國際有限公司｜初版一刷 2009 年 10 月 13 日｜二版一刷 2015 年 02 月 24 日

Printed in Taiwan

ISBN：978-986-6031-65-6　版權所有‧翻印必究　售價：280 元

目錄　Contents

找出自在法門 任創意無限發想

鄭緯笙（Vista）

提起「創意」，我的腦袋裡就會浮現很多畫面。其實，很久以前我就讀過《創意，從無到有》這本看起來輕薄短小但內容卻擲地有聲的好書。幾乎可以篤定地說，搞創意的人不能不好好拜讀這本大作，我也相信大家可以從閱讀的過程中，理解創意是如何生成的？

本書作者楊傑美（James Webb Young）已經逝世屆滿四十二年了，儘管廣告、創意的領域發展迅速，幾乎可以用「一日千里」來形容。但這一切從未減損過《創意，從無到有》（*A Technique for Producing Ideas*）這本書的權威性，甚至隨著時代的演進，這本小書中所提到的某些原則（好比專注），更受到當今許多專家、學者的推崇。

出生於西元一八八六年的楊傑美，是美國知名的廣告大師，他在智威湯遜廣告公司（JWT）任職超過半個世紀，曾出版《廣告人日記》（*The Diary of an Ad Man*）、《創意，從無到有》（*A Technique for Producing Ideas*），以及《如何成為廣告人？》（*How to Become an Advertising Man*）等三部經典的廣告學著作。

一九三九年時,廣告大師楊傑美首度在芝加哥大學開給商學院研究生的廣告學課堂上,發表和《創意,從無到有》有關的內容,之後於一九六五年正式集結出版這本書,也立刻受到歐美等國廣告、公關產業菁英的追捧。一時之間洛陽紙貴,楊傑美的觀點吸引了許多廣告、創業圈人士,不但幫他個人掙得了許多殊榮、獎項,大家更將書中所提到的若干原則奉為圭臬。

很多人都羨慕創意人精采豐富的生活,但也好奇他們如何有源源不絕的靈感?創意究竟是怎麼來的,楊傑美試著用五個步驟來幫大家歸納:首先要蒐集大量的資料,然後再消化吸收,並且能夠讓潛意識為你工作。之後,便可迸發創意,再將創意作最後的修正,以符合實際的用途。

以我自己來說,因為熱愛創作,也把寫作視為主要的興趣和工作,所以我很早就知道專注和鍛鍊心智的重要性。我訓練自己戒除依賴靈感,轉而從日常生活中去觀察大量的事物,並積累、內化成自我的創意資料庫。一旦不受靈感的羈絆,那麼創作就可以行雲流水、恣意揮灑。

我很同意作者所提到的，創意生產誠然是一門藝術。因此，我們最應該要學習的並不是到哪裡去尋找特定的靈感，而是如何訓練心智熟稔創意生產的方法，並且要能夠充分掌握所有創意背後的基本原則。

話雖如此，但我們也不用把創意想得太玄了！因為大師也告訴我們，創意不過是舊元素的重新組合。想想當初 iPhone 問世的時候，不是也有人譏諷地說「這個產品沒什麼？」，只不過就是結合了隨身聽、電話、GPS 導航和網路等等機制而已。但現在大家也知曉，困難的往往不是點子本身，而是如何具體落實想法，並且完美地滿足消費者的各種需求。

如果你還不清楚如何生產創意，我覺得也可參照楊傑美大師的建議，從尋找事物間的脈絡與關連性開始：試著拉高自己的視野，再從點、線到面去找出各種細節，進而構連出一個「立體」的架構。

觀察，不但是創意人最重要的心理習慣，也是很基本的一門功課。當我們心中已經有了藍圖，創意的生成自然也就可以隨手拈來！

誠摯地跟大家推薦這本好書，希望大家在創意發想的過程中，都能找到自在的法門。

本文作者為臺灣電子商務創業聯誼會理事長
http://vista.tw
http://www.taiwanec.net/

這是一本很小的大書

王艾莉

我在大學教書時，時常會有人來問我，設計到底有沒有課本？有沒有可以 follow 的程式或步驟？我一開始都會很篤定地回答：「沒有」，但後來仔細地想了想，設計的過程其實是有一定的步驟的，只是我們不知道如何把它統整成一套系統。而許多設計師或知名設計公司所發表的設計方法，往往只著重於發想方式（Brainstorming），除了沒有一個完整的過程外，那些發想方式，感覺上也與我的有些出入。

我自己的思考方式其實有點難以形容，不過思考的過程有時跟煮湯很像：首先我會去市面及網路上搜刮各類的資料及元素，接著開始結合一些比較「登對」的概念，然後把它們「暫時忘掉」一段時間，讓這些概念自個兒留在腦袋裡「滾」個幾天。而在這幾天內，我只會偶而想起這些破碎零散的 ideas，然後就在某天不經意的時候，一個令自己滿意的 IDEA 就會突然從腦海中蹦出！有時 IDEA 實在來得太過突然，可能剛好在走路，或是洗澡洗到一半，這時就得趕緊拿起手機記下來，否則之後要是忘了，肯定會後悔莫及。

楊傑美（James Webb Young）的《創意，從無到有》（*A Technique for Producing Ideas*）於一九六五年第一次出版，可以說是本老書了！外觀薄又輕巧，內容的敘述方式也很簡單易懂，所以我不到半天就把整本書看完了！他將設計過程分成五大步驟，清楚地敘述並舉例每個階段該完成的事情，因此書齡老歸老，我一念完的感想就是「THIS IS IT!」彷彿有人幫我把我心中想的設計過程給記錄了下來似的。

這本書能讓你廣泛的應用在各種不同的創意領域中，只要細細品味，便能讓你深入地了解從頭到尾、每個步驟的細節。別光看體積和頁數，其實它是本很小的大書！

本文作者為王艾莉設計負責人

Foreword

**By Keith Reinhard, Chairman,
DDB Worldwide**

How can a book first published in the 1940s be important to creative people on today's cutting edge? By answering the question that inspired James Webb Young to write this remarkable little volume in the first place: "How do you get ideas?" The blank page or screen that awaits a transforming idea today is just as intimidating as ever. Maybe more so, because our advanced environments demand even better ideas and more of them. The steps laid down by Young are the surest path to that incomparable thrill of discovery the author describes as the "Eureka! I have it!" stage.

When I first encountered this book, I was still a working creative director. I had never heard of James Webb Young but, like most other creative people in advertising, I was a fan and follower of Bill Bernbach, who revolutionized the ad world in the late fifties and sixties with his rule-breaking work for a number of brands, most notable the Volkswagen Beetle. When I saw that Bill had written a foreword to the book, I knew I should check it out.

奇斯・雷哈德
DDB 廣告公司董事長

一本在一九四○年代首次出版的書，對今日的創意工作者而言為什麼還如此重要？因為，它回答了一個重要的問題：「創意是怎麼來的？」本書的作者楊傑美（James Webb Young），就是為了回答該問題而寫出這本了不起的小書。今天，要為一張空白的紙或空白的螢幕賦予高明的創意，不但跟過去一樣困難，甚至有過之而無不及。因為，在今天的環境下，你提出的創意不但要比以前更好、還要更多。所幸，作者在本書中揭示了激發創意的幾個步驟，只要你能切實加以實踐，你一定能發現令你驚喜無比的創意，到達作者所描述「啊！我找到了！」的階段。

第一次看到這本書時，我還是個創意總監。雖然沒聽過楊傑美這個名字，但我和廣告業絕大多數的創意工作者一樣，是威廉・伯恩巴克（William Bernbach）的崇拜者和追隨者。伯恩巴克在五○年代末和六○年代改革了廣告界，他打破成規，為許多品牌打造出煥然一新的廣告，其中最著名的是他為福斯金龜車（Volkswagen Beetle）所做的廣告。當我看到伯恩巴克為這本書寫推薦序時，我知道，這本書我一定要找來看看。

What I found was the most concise and illuminating description of the creative process I had ever read. I sent out at once for enough copies to supply the entire creative department, and since then, I've handed out hundreds more.

For creative people just getting started, Young offers both guidance and the assurance that coming up with an idea is a process, not an accident. For those more experienced, Young comforts us with the knowledge that what we might have thought was pure intuition is actually a series of steps that can be described and taught and repeated over and over again. And, should this little book fall into the hands of those who say "I've never had an idea in my life," they just might surprise themselves.

結果，我看到了一本談創意過程最精簡扼要也最具啟發性的描述。我馬上為整個創意部門的同仁訂購這本書；在那之後，我還送出好幾百本給其他人。

對於剛從事創意工作的人而言，這本書除了具指引作用，還能夠提醒他們：創意的生產是個過程，而非瞎貓碰到死耗子的結果。對於入行較久的人來說，這本書則可以帶來慰藉：原來，我們一直認為純屬直覺的東西，其實是一連串步驟的結果，而且，這些步驟是可以被描述、被教導、被再三重複的。最後，如果你認為自己此生從來與創意無緣，那麼我要告訴你，這本書會讓你大吃一驚。

Foreword

By William Bernbach, Chairman,
Worldwide and Chief Executive Officer,
Doyle Dane Bernbach Inc.

James Webb Young conveys in his little book something more valuable than the most learned and detailed texts on the subject of advertising. For he is talking about the soul of a piece of communications and not merely the flesh and bones. He is talking about the idea. A chemist can inexpensively put together a human body. What he can't do is spark it with life. Mr. Young writes about the creative spark, the ideas, which bring spirit and life to an advertisement. Nothing is more important to the practice of our craft.

Mr. Young is in the tradition of some of our greatest thinkers when he describes the workings of the creative process. It is a tribute to him that such scientific giants as Bertrand Russell and Albert Einstein have written similarly on this subject. They agree that knowledge is basic to good creative thinking but that it is not enough, that this knowledge must be digested and eventually emerge in the form of fresh, new combinations and relationships. Einstein refers to this as intuition, which he considers the only path to new insights.

威廉・伯恩巴克
恆美廣告公司前董事長兼執行長

這本書雖然輕薄短小，作者楊傑美所傳達的精神，卻比市面上許多最艱深、最詳盡的廣告書籍還要更有價值。因為，他談的不只是廣告文宣的皮肉，而是它的靈魂，是創意。化學家無須耗費太多資金就能架構出一副人體，卻無法賦予它生命的火花。創意—也就是賦予廣告精神與生命的火花　—則是本書所探討的主題。從事廣告這一行，沒有什麼比這更重要的了。

由於本書談的是創意的過程，從這一點來看，作者繼承了自古以來某些最偉大思想家的傳統。包括羅素（Bertrand Russell）、愛因斯坦（Albert Einstein）等科學巨擘在內，都曾經為文探討過類似的主題。他們一致認為：知識，是優秀的創意性思考的基礎，但這樣還不夠，因為，知識必須被消化吸收，再透過新的排列組合，以新鮮的形式問世，才可能產生真正的創意。愛因斯坦稱這樣的東西為直覺，他還認為，這是產生新洞見的唯一途徑。

The quality of the ideas you get cannot be guaranteed, and James Webb Young would, I am sure, be the first one to tell you this. That quality would be the result of all the forces in your life that have played on you, including your genes. But you will be making the most of those forces and all your natural equipment if you follow the procedures he outlines so simply and lucidly.

We are indebted to Mr. Young for getting to the heart of the matter. The result of many years of work in advertising have proved to him that the key element in communications success is the production of relevant and dramatic ideas. He not only makes this point vividly for us but shows us the road to that goal.

但，創意的好壞，沒有人能夠保證。這一點，我相信作者一定非常同意。你這輩子所受到的各種影響，包括你的遺傳基因，都會左右你的創意的品質。儘管如此，作者將創意生產的程序分析得極為簡單明瞭，只要你遵照他敘述的步驟，你一定能夠將你所受到的各種影響和你的天生稟賦發揮得淋漓盡致。

感謝作者，如此直接地為我們點出了創意生產的核心精神。多年的廣告工作經驗讓他清楚體認到，一份廣告文宣的成功與否，關鍵在於文宣背後的創意是不是具有關連性和戲劇性。作者不但清楚說明這一點，也為我們指出達到該目標的道路所在。

Prefatory Note

These thoughts were first presented to graduate students in advertising at the School of Business of the University of Chicago and later before several gatherings of active advertising practitioners. This accounts for the informal tone.

The subject is properly one which belongs to the professional psychologist, which I am not. This treatment of it, therefore, can have value only as an expression of the personal experience of one who has had to earn his living by producing what were alleged to be ideas.

It was first prepared one Sunday afternoon when I had to consider what I should say to a Monday class. No literature on the subject was at the moment available; nor had I any recollection of having seen any. Since then many readers of this book have called my attention to writings on the same subject, from different areas of experience; and there have been published several recent books with something worthwhile to say on this topic. On the last page of this edition I have listed three which I have found stimulating.

James Webb Young
Rancho de la Cañada, Peña Blanca, New Mexico
July 1960

前言

本書的內容，最初是發表在芝加哥大學商學院研究生的廣告學課堂上，後來又在廣告同業的聚會中發表過幾次，因此書中的筆調是比較隨性的。

嚴格說來，本書的主題屬於專業心理學的領域。由於我並非心理學家，因此本書充其量只能算是我這個以生產「創意」為生的人的經驗談。

這本書的誕生，最初源於某星期天的下午，我正為了週一的某堂課要上些什麼而傷透腦筋。當時，並無任何現成的相關文獻可供參考，我印象中也沒看過任何這方面的資料。然而，當本書出版了以後，許多讀者都熱心地告訴我，哪裡可以找到相關的文章，而類似的書籍也在之後幾年陸續問世。本次趁著改版之際，我在書末列出了三本我個人認為特別值得一讀的著作。

楊傑美
新墨西哥州培雅布蘭卡，卡亞達牧場
一九六〇年七月

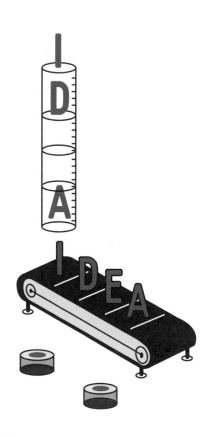

「創意是怎麼來的？」
生產創意與銷售創意，這中間的過程是什麼呢？

緣起

How It Started

How It Started

One day in my last year as an advertising agency executive in Chicago I had a telephone call from the western advertising manager of a well-known magazine.

He asked if he could see me immediately on a matter of importance. Shortly thereafter he arrived in my office, somewhat out of breath.

"We are having a meeting today," he said, "of our entire western sales staff. Its purpose is to discuss how we can improve our selling.

"In our discussions we have tried to analyze the selling methods of other successful publications and salesmen. And among these we have been particularly impressed by the success of Mr. Kobler in his selling of the *American Weekly*.

那是我在芝加哥某廣告公司擔任主管的最後一年，有一天，我接到某知名雜誌西部地區廣告部經理打來的電話。

他表示有重要的事情想請教，希望能馬上會面。過沒多久，他氣喘吁吁地出現在我的辦公室裡。

「是這樣的，」他說：「我們今天召集西部地區所有業務同仁開了個會，討論如何增加銷售量。

「會中，我們分析其他成功的出版品和業務員的行銷手法。結果，卡伯勒先生（Mr. Kobler）的《美國週刊》（*American Weekly*）銷售成績最讓我們印象深刻。

"After studying just why he is so successful we have come to the conclusion that it all rests on just one thing: he doesn't sell space; he sells Ideas.

"And so," he continued, with enthusiasm, "we have decided that that is just what we are going to do. From here on we are not going to sell space at all. Beginning tomorrow morning every single one of us is going to sell **Ideas!**"

I said I thought that was just dandy but wondered what it was that he wanted to discuss with me.

"Well," he said, somewhat ruefully, "we could see that what we ought to do is to sell ideas, all right. But after that we sort of got stuck.

"What we are not clear about is just how to get ideas.

"So I said maybe you could tell us, and that is what I am here for.

「經過研究之後，我們一致認為，卡伯勒先生成功的原因只有一個：他賣的不是版面，而是創意。

「於是，」我的客人繼續興致勃勃地說：「我們決定見賢思齊。從現在起，我們不再銷售版面。明早開始，我們每個人都將致力於銷售**創意**！」

我告訴他，這個想法很棒，但也不禁懷疑，他到底想跟我談什麼呢？

「是這樣的，」他有點無奈地說：「我們知道自己應該朝銷售創意的方向而努力，但我們到這裡就卡住了。

「困擾我們的是，不曉得該如何生產創意。

「於是我告訴公司的同仁說，也許你可以給我們答案，而這也是我來此的目的。

"You have produced a lot of advertising ideas. Just how do you get them? The boys are waiting for me to come back and tell them."

Now I know that if I had not been so flattered by this question, and if my questioner had not been so obviously serious in asking it, I would have had a hearty fit of laughing at this point.

I thought at the time that I had never heard a funnier or more naive question. And I was completely unable to give any helpful answer to it.

But it struck me afterward that maybe the question **"How do you get ideas?"** wasn't as silly as it sounded. Maybe there was some answer to it. And off and on I thought about it.

「你創造過很多廣告點子。請問，這些點子是怎麼來的？我的同事還在等我回去給他們答覆呢。」

現在回想，當下要不是我被這位先生給捧昏頭了，要不是他的發問態度如此認真，我應該會捧腹大笑才是。

因為我覺得，我從來沒聽過比這更可笑、更天真的問題了。我無法給他任何有用的答案。

但，事後我卻驚覺，「**創意是怎麼來的？**」這個問題，說到底並不愚蠢。這個問題，或許確實是有答案的。於是我開始反覆思索。

創意的生產，跟福特汽車的製程一樣明確，一樣得仰賴「生產線」
需要遵循一套學得起來、也可以控制的「運作技術」

從經驗歸納而來的公式

The Formula of Experience

The Formula of Experience

An idea, I thought, has some of that mysterious quality which romance lends to tales of the sudden appearance of islands in the South Seas.

There, according to ancient mariners, in spots where the charts showed only deep blue sea, there would suddenly appear a lovely atoll above the surface of the waters. An air of magic hung about it.

And so it is, I thought, with Ideas. They appear just as suddenly above the surface of the mind—and with that same air of magic and unaccountability.

But the scientist knows that the South Sea atoll is the work of countless, unseen coral builders, working below the surface of the sea.

And so I asked myself: "Is an idea, too, like this? Is it only the final result of a long series of unseen idea-building processes which go on beneath the surface of the conscious mind?

從經驗歸納而來的公式

創意這東西，我總認為，具有某種神祕的色彩，就好比傳奇故事裡突然出現在南太平洋上的島嶼一樣。

根據古代水手流傳下來的故事，在那些航海圖上標示為深藍色的海域，有時候會忽然冒出美麗的環礁，其四周瀰漫著奇幻的氛圍。

我想創意也是如此。它也會突然浮出意識的表面，而且，它的出現，跟南太平洋上的環礁一樣神奇、一樣叫人匪夷所思。

但科學家知道，出現在南太平洋上的環礁，事實上是海面下無數的珊瑚經年累月所形成的。

於是我不禁自忖：「創意是否也是如此？創意，會不會就只是一連串看不見的過程在意識表面底下長期醞釀之後的結果？

"If so, can these processes be identified, so that they can consciously be followed and utilized? In short, can a formula or technique be developed in answer to the question: **How do you get ideas?**"

What I now propose to you is the result of a long-time pondering of these questions and of close observation of the work of idea-producing men with whom I have had associations.

This has brought me to the conclusion that the production of ideas is just as definite a process as the production of Fords; that the production of ideas, too, runs on an assembly line; that in this production the mind follows an **operative technique** which can be learned and controlled; and that its effective use is just as much a matter of **practice in the technique** as is the effective use of any tool.

「如果真是如此，這些過程可以被指認出來，讓人有意識地加以遵循和運用嗎？簡言之，我們能不能發展出一套公式或技巧，以解決這個問題：**你如何生產創意？**」

現在呈現在各位眼前的，便是我長期思索這些問題，並仔細觀察共事過的創意夥伴的工作情形之後，所得出的結果。

經由上述的思索和觀察，我得出的結論是：創意的生產，跟福特汽車的製程一樣明確；它同樣得仰賴生產線。在創意生產的過程中，我們的心智也需要遵循一套可以被學習、可以被控制的**運作技術**（operative technique）；而且，這套技術跟任何工具一樣，必須多加練習才會**熟能生巧**。

If you ask me why I am willing to give away the valuable formula of this discovery I will confide to you that experience has taught me two things about it:

First, the formula is so simple to state that few who hear it really believe in it.

Second, while simple to state, it actually requires the hardest kind of intellectual work to follow, so that not all who accept it use it.

Thus I broadcast this formula with no real fear of glutting the market in which I make my living.

要是你問我，這套公式如此珍貴，為什麼我還願意公開與他人分享？因為，我從經驗中學會了兩件事。

第一，這套公式太簡單了，簡單到許多人覺得難以置信。

第二，這套公式說來容易，做起來卻相當困難，你必須下苦功進行心智的鍛鍊才行，因此，有些人雖然相信，卻無法付諸實踐。

正因為這兩個因素，我並不擔心自己的飯碗會被搶走，所以才放心將這套公式廣為宣傳。

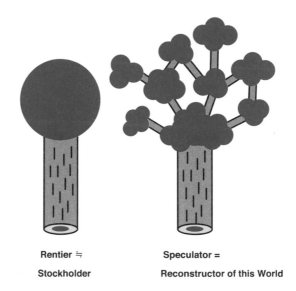

Rentier ≒
Stockholder

Speculator =
Reconstructor of this World

投機者 Speculator = Reconstructor of this World
不斷專注於新組合的可能性，具備創意生產的能力

股東 Rentier ≒ Stockholder
喜歡一成不變的穩定生活、缺乏想像力、個性保守，往往會被投機者操弄

**A Technique
for Producing Ideas**

帕雷托
法則

The Pareto Theory

The Pareto Theory

Now, we all know men of whom we have said: "He never had an idea in his life."

That saying brings us face to face with the first real question about this subject. Even assuming that there may be a technique for producing ideas, is everybody capable of using it? Or is there, in addition, some special ability for producing ideas which, after all, you must be born with—like a color sense or tone sense or card sense?

One answer to that question is suggested in the work *Mind and Society* by the great Italian sociologist Pareto.

Pareto thought that all the world could be divided into two main types of people. These types he called, in the French in which he wrote, the *speculator* and the *rentier*.

帕雷托法則

談到創意，相信每個人都曾如此評論過別人：「他這個人，這輩子從來沒提出過什麼創意。」

這樣的說法，點出了關於創意的第一個大哉問。假使創意生產真有所謂的技術可言，那麼，這件事是不是每個人都辦得到呢？又或者需要某些特殊的天賦，如色感、音感、牌感之類的？

關於這個問題，偉大的義大利社會學家帕雷托[1]，在他的著作《心靈與社會》（*Mind and Society*）中，提出了一個可能的答案。

帕雷托認為，世上的人大略可分為兩類，他分別以法文「speculator」與「rentier」稱之。

---

1 編註： Vilfredo Pareto，1848-1923。義大利企業家、社會學家、經濟學家，以及哲學家。他在經濟學領域提出幾項重要貢獻，尤其是收入分配的研究及個人選擇的分析。

In this classification *speculator* is a term used somewhat in the sense of our word "speculative." The *speculator* is the speculative type of person. And the distinguishing characteristic of this type, according to Pareto, is that he is **constantly preoccupied with the possibilities of new combinations.**

Please hold that italicized definition in mind, because we shall return to it later. Note particularly that word *pre-occupied*, with its brooding quality.

Pareto includes among the persons of this speculative type not only the business enterprisers—those who deal with financial and business schemes—but those engaged with inventions of every sort and with what he calls "political and diplomatic reconstructions."

In short, the type includes all those persons in any field who (like our President Roosevelt) can not let well enough alone and who speculate on how to change it.

其中的「speculator」，大約可翻譯成「投機者」。帕雷托認為，這類人的典型特徵為：**不斷專注於新組合的可能性。**

上述定義，請各位謹記在心，因為我們稍後會再談到。尤其是「專注」二字，更是這類人的突出特質。

根據帕雷托的看法，投機者不僅包括創業家——他們必須處理財務上和商業上的經營擘劃——也包括各式各樣的發明家，以及他所謂的「政治和外交上的重建者」。

簡言之，一個人如果不輕易滿足於現狀，而總是亟思改變之道（如美國總統羅斯福），則不管他處在哪個領域，都可以被歸為這一類。

The term used by Pareto to describe the other type, the *rentier*, is translated into English as the stockholder—though he sounds more like the bag holder to me. Such people, he says, are the routine, steady-going, unimaginative, conserving people, whom the *speculator* manipulates.

Whatever we may think of the adequacy of this theory of Pareto's as an entire explanation of social groups, I think we all recognize that these two types of human beings do exist. Whether they were born that way, or whether their environment and training made them that way, is beside the point. They **are.**

This being the case I suppose it must be true that there are large numbers of people whom no technique for producing ideas will ever help.

至於另外一類人，帕雷托用「rentier」來加以形容。「rentier」
這個字翻譯成中文，大概近似於股東的意思——但在我看來，
這些人較像是抱著雞蛋水餃股的股東。帕雷托形容，這類人喜
歡一成不變的穩定生活、缺乏想像力、個性保守，而且往往被
投機者所操縱。

無論你認不認同帕雷托這樣的分類，我想大家應該都同意，這
兩類人確實存在。至於這些人是天生如此，抑或是後天的環境
或訓練造就而成，則非我們討論的重點。重點是，這兩類人**確
實存在**。

既然如此，我猜，這世上確實有不少人是無論如何都學不會創
意生產的。

But it seems to me that the important point for our purpose is that the **speculators**, or reconstructors of this world, are a very large group. Theirs at least is the inherent capacity to produce ideas, and it is by no means such a rare capacity. And so, while perhaps not all God's chilluns got wings, enough have for each of us to hope that we may be among those that have.

At any rate, I propose to assume that if a man (or woman) is at all fascinated by advertising it is probably because he is among the reconstructors of this world. Therefore he has some creative powers; and these powers, like others, may be increased by making a deliberate effort to do so and by mastering a technique for their better use.

但，就本文的探討目的而言，重點是，所謂的**投機者**或世界的重建者，人數是相當龐大的。他們天生具備創意生產的能力，而且這份能力並不罕見。因此，儘管不是每個上帝的子民都擁有翅膀[2]，但我們仍能期待自己正是擁有翅膀的人。

總之，我想說的是，一個人只要對廣告感興趣，他（她）或許就是這個世界的重建者之一。也就是說，人具有某種創造力，而這種能力和其他能力一樣，是可以透過刻意的努力和熟練的技巧而進步的。

---

2 編註：出自尤金 · 奧尼爾（Eugene O'Neill，1888-1953，美國劇作家及諾貝爾文學獎得主）的一部以黑人命運為主題的劇作 ——《上帝的兒女都有翅膀》（*All God's Chillun Got Wings*）。講述一椿發生在黑人男性和白人女性之間的不幸婚姻故事，闡明種族偏見對美國黑人和白人民族共同的破壞力量，同時也表明對美國黑人民族悲慘處境的同情、理解，以及對美國殘酷的種族隔離環境的譴責。

創意生成的藝術＝熟悉方法＋掌握原則

鍛鍊心智

Training the Mind

Training the Mind

Assuming, then, that we have some natural capacity for the creation of ideas, we come to the practical question: "What are the means of developing it?"

In learning any art the important things to learn are, first, Principles, and second, Method. This is true of the art of producing ideas.

Particular bits of knowledge are nothing, because they are made up of what Dr. Robert Hutchins once called **rapidly aging facts**. Principles and method are everything.

Thus in advertising we may know the names of types, how much engravings cost, what the rates and closing dates are in a thousand publications; we may know enough grammar and rhetoric to confound a schoolteacher and enough names of television artists to hold our own at a

鍛鍊心智

假使我們天生具有某種創意能力，那我們不免要問一個實際的問題：「這種能力要如何培養？」

學習任何技藝，有兩樣東西最為重要，第一是原則，第二是方法。創意的生產也不例外。

至於特定的知識，則如同羅伯特・霍金斯博士[1]所說，是**快速老化的事實**，因此無關緊要。原則和方法才是一切。

也就是說，就算你從事廣告業，知道各種字體的名稱，曉得各種版面的價格，清楚一千份刊物的售價和發行日期；你的文法和修辭的素養或許遠勝許多中小學的老師，也舉得出夠多演藝人員的名字，能夠在媒體業的雞尾酒會上大顯身手；但，要是你不了解廣告背後的原則和方法，就算你懂這麼多東西，你仍然稱不上是廣告人。

---

1 編註： Dr. Robert Hutchins，1899-1977，是美國著名的教育哲學家，曾擔任耶魯大學法學院院長（1927-1929），以及芝加哥大學校長（1945-1951）。

broadcaster's cocktail party; we may know all these things and still not be an advertising man, because we have no understanding of the principles and fundamental methods by which advertising works.

On the other hand, we may know none of these things but have insight into advertising principles and method, so that by employing technicians to help us we may produce advertising results. Thus we sometimes see a manufacturer or merchant who is a better advertising man than his advertising agent or manager.

So with the art of producing ideas. What is most valuable to know is not where to look for a particular idea, but how to train the mind in the **method** by which all ideas are produced and how to grasp the **principles** which are at the source of all ideas.

相反地，有些人雖然不懂上述所有事務，卻深諳廣告的原則和方法，因此只要聘請一些技術人員就可以達成廣告效益。這就是為什麼，我們有時候會看到比廣告代理商更懂廣告的業主。

創意生產的藝術也是如此。因此你最應該要學習的並不是到哪裡去尋找特定的靈感，而是如何訓練你的心智熟稔創意生產的**方法**，並掌握所有創意背後的基本**原則**。

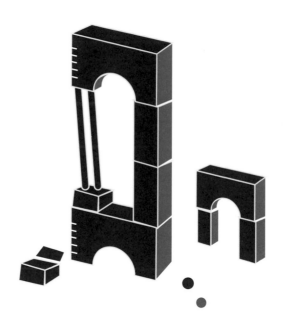

「創意，不過是舊元素的重新組合」

看到不同事物間的關連性

↓

找出普遍性原則

↓

將舊素材重新組合，由舊翻出新點子

5

A Technique
for Producing Ideas

重新組合
舊有的元素

Combining Old Elements

Combining Old Elements

With regard to the general principles which underlie the production of ideas, it seems to me that there are two which are important.

The first of these has already been touched upon in the quotation from Pareto: namely, that **an idea is nothing more nor less than a new combination of old elements.**

This is, perhaps, the most important fact in connection with the production of ideas. However, I want to leave the elaboration of it until we come to a discussion of method. Then we can see the importance of this fact more clearly, through the application of it.

The second important principle involved is that the capacity to bring old elements into new combinations depends largely on the ability to see relationships.

重新組合舊有的元素

在我看來，創意的生產有兩個最重要的一般性原則。

第一個原則，我在介紹帕雷托法則時就已經大略談到，那就是：
創意不過是舊元素的重新組合。

這一點，或許是有關創意生產的最重要事實。不過，我希望等
到介紹方法時再進行更深入的探討。屆時，透過這項原則的運
用，我們將更能體會這個事實的重要性。

第二個原則談的是，要將舊元素重新組合，主要有賴於以下這
項能力：能看到不同事物間的關連性。

Here, I suspect, is where minds differ to the greatest degree when it comes to the production of ideas. To some minds each fact is a separate bit of knowledge. To others it is a link in a chain of knowledge. It has relationships and similarities. It is not so much a fact as it is an illustration of a general law applying to a whole series of facts.

An illustration of this might be taken from a relationship between advertising and psychiatry. At first blush it might be hoped that there is no relationship! But the psychiatrists have discovered the profound influence which words have in the lives of their patients—words as symbols of emotional experiences.

And now Dr. Harold Lasswell has carried over these word-symbol studies of the psychiatrists to the field of political action and shown how word-symbols are used with the same emotional force in propaganda.

這一點，我想正是每個人在提及創意生產時，思考上最不一樣的地方。對某些人而言，A 事實和 B 事實是互不相干的；但是在某些人看來，A 事實和 B 事實之間卻存在了某些關連性或相似性。每個事實的背後都有一個普遍性的原則，而且，這個原則是適用於很多事實的。

這一點，或許可以用廣告和心理治療之間的關連性來舉例說明。乍看之下，這兩者之間怎麼可能有關連呢？但，心理治療師發現，語言，在病人的生命中發揮了非常深遠的影響力——語言是情緒經驗的表徵。

後來，哈洛德·拉斯威爾博士[1] 將心理治療師所做的這些關於語言象徵的研究，引進政治學領域，證明了語言象徵所發揮的情緒感染力，在政治宣傳上同樣威力強大。

---

1 編註： Harold Lasswell，1902-1978。美國耶魯大學著名政治學家和傳播學家。

To a mind which is quick to see relationships several ideas will occur, fruitful for advertising, about this use of words as symbols. Is this, then, why the change of one word in a headline can make as much as 50 percent difference in advertising response? Can words, studied as emotional symbols, yield better advertising education than words studied as parts of rhetoric? What is the one word-symbol which will best arouse the emotion with which I wish this particular advertisement to be charged? And so on.

The point is, of course, that when relationships of this kind are seen they lead to the extraction of a general principle. This general principle, when grasped, suggests the key to a new application, a new combination, and the result is an idea.

一旦了解語言是情緒的象徵，敏於覺察事物間關連性的人，此時可能會在腦海中浮現出好幾個有助於做廣告的想法。譬如，為何有時候廣告標題只要更動一個字，效果就相差了50%？在教育廣告人時，與其將語言當成修辭學來研究，不如把它視為情緒的象徵，是否這樣訓練的效果會更好？有哪個字詞象徵，最能夠讓閱聽人產生我希望這則廣告所引發的情緒感受？諸如此類的想法。

當然，這背後的重點是，一旦看到了事物間的關連性，你或許就能從中找出一個普遍性的原則。一旦掌握了這普遍性的原則，你或許就會想到如何將舊的素材予以重新應用、重新組合，進而創造出新的點子。

Consequently the habit of mind which leads to a search for relationships between facts becomes of the highest importance in the production of ideas. Now this habit of mind can undoubtedly be cultivated. I venture to suggest that, for the advertising man, one of the best ways to cultivate it is by study in the social sciences. A book like Veblen's *Theory of the Leisure Class* or Riesman's *The Lonely Crowd*, therefore, becomes a better book about advertising than most books about advertising.

因此，要生產創意，習於去尋找事物間的關連性，是最最重要的心理習慣。還好，這項習慣是可以培養的。我認為，對廣告工作者而言，要培養這樣的心理習慣，最好的方法是研讀社會學著作。如范伯倫（Veblen）的《有閒階級論》[2]或黎士曼（Riesman）的《寂寞的群眾》[3]，這些書比大多數的廣告學書籍更能夠教你學會做廣告。

2 編註： Thorstein Veblen，1857-1929。美國經濟學家，制度經濟學的創立者。*Theory of the Leisure Class*，中文版由左岸文化出版。

3 編註： David Riesman，1909-2002。美國社會學家及教育家。 *The Lonely Crowd*，中文版由桂冠圖書出版。

所謂的創意，往往就是將產品和消費者的特定資訊，
以及生活或時事的一般性資訊，加以重新組合的結果

創意就是
新的組合

Ideas Are New Combinations

Ideas Are New Combinations

With these two general principles in mind—the principle that an idea is a new combination, and the principle that the ability to make new combinations is heightened by an ability to see relationships—with these in mind let us now look at the actual method or procedure by which ideas are produced.

As I said before, what I am now about to contend is that in the production of ideas the mind follows a method which is just as definite as the method by which, say, Fords are produced.

In other words, that there is a technique for the use of the mind for this purpose; that whenever an idea is produced this technique is followed, consciously or unconsciously; and that this technique can consciously be cultivated and the ability of the mind to produce ideas thereby increased.

創意就是新的組合

上一章介紹了創意生產的兩大原則——創意就是將舊的元素重新排列組合；有辦法看到不同事物間的關連性，你就越有能力創造出新的組合。在知道這兩大原則之後，接下來讓我們看看創意生產的實際方法或程序。

一如先前所說，我在此主張的是，在生產創意的過程中，我們的心智會遵循一套特定的方法，而這個方法，就像福特汽車的製造過程一樣具體明確。

換言之，要達成生產創意的目的，其實是有方法可以遵循的；也就是說，任何創意之所以能夠誕生，當事人一定會在過程中有意無意間使用到這套方法。而且，這套方法可以有意識地加以培養，進而提高我們的創意生產力。

This technique of the mind follows five steps. I am sure that you will all recognize them individually. But the important thing is to recognize their relationship and to grasp the fact that the mind follows these five steps in definite order—that by no possibility can one of them be taken before the preceding one is completed, if an idea is to be produced.

The first of these steps is for the mind to gather its raw material.

That, I am sure, will strike you as a simple and obvious truth. Yet it is really amazing to what degree this step is ignored in practice.

Gathering raw material in a real way is not as simple as it sounds. It is such a terrible chore that we are constantly trying to dodge it. The time that ought to be spent in material gathering is spent in wool gathering. Instead of working systematically at the job of gathering raw material we sit around hoping for inspiration to strike us. When we do that we are trying to get the mind to take the fourth step in the idea-producing process while we dodge the preceding steps.

總的來說，這套方法共包含五個步驟。這五個步驟若分開來看，相信各位都不難了解。重點是，你必須認清這五個步驟之間的關係，了解到這些步驟必須依序進行，不能前後顛倒，才能成功地生產出創意來。

這五個步驟的第一步，是替你的腦袋蒐集原始素材。

各位大概會覺得，這不是廢話嗎？但我要告訴大家，事實上這個步驟經常遭到忽略。

蒐集原始素材聽起來容易，其實不然。這個工作太枯燥了，很多人總是敬而遠之。結果，你應該蒐集素材的時間，都被你拿來胡思亂想，做白日夢去了。因此，我們並沒有用系統化的方式進行資料蒐集的工作，反倒枯坐在那兒等著靈感自動送上門。換句話說，我們只想直接跳到第四步驟，而略過前面幾個步驟。

The materials which must be gathered are of two kinds: they are specific and they are general.

In advertising, the specific materials are those relating to the product and the people to whom you propose to sell it. We constantly talk about the importance of having an intimate knowledge of the product and the consumer, but in fact we seldom work at it.

This, I suppose, is because a real knowledge of a product, and of people in relation to it, is not easy to come by. Getting it is something like the process which was recommended to De Maupassant as the way to learn to write. "Go out into the streets of Paris," he was told by an older writer, "and pick out a cab driver. He will look to you very much like every other cab driver. But study him until you can describe him so that he is seen in your description to be an individual, different from every other cab driver in the world."

要蒐集的素材，大致可分成兩種：特定的和一般的。

在廣告工作中，所謂特定的素材，指的是那些和產品或你打算推銷的對象直接相關的資訊。許多廣告人口頭上經常說，徹底了解產品和消費者有多重要，事實上卻往往無法做到。

為什麼呢？我認為一個很重要的原因在於，要真正了解一項產品以及與該產品相關的人，並不是件容易的事。這，有點像是十九世紀法國文豪莫泊桑（De Maupassant）在開始學寫作時，從一位前輩作家[1]口中得到的建議：「到巴黎的街上走一走，隨便挑一位馬車夫進行觀察。一開始你可能覺得，這位馬車夫和其他馬車夫沒什麼兩樣啊。但你必須不斷觀察，直到你能夠寫出他的個人特色，讓他不同於世界上其他的馬車夫為止。」

---

1 編註： 此處所指的是福樓拜（Gustave Flaubert, 1821-1880），法國十九世紀最嚴格的文體家，寫實主義文學泰斗。著有《包法利夫人》、《情感教育》等膾炙人口的作品。

This is the real meaning of that trite talk about getting an intimate knowledge of a product and its consumers. Most of us stop too soon in the process of getting it. If the surface differences are not striking we assume that there are no differences. But if we go deeply enough, or far enough, we nearly always find that between every product and some consumers there is an individuality of relationship which may lead to an idea.

Thus, for example, I could cite you the advertising for a well-known soap. At first there appeared nothing to say about it that had not been said for many soaps. But a study was made of the relation of soap to skin and hair—a study which resulted in a fair-sized book on the subject. And out of this book came copy ideas for five years of advertising; ideas which multiplied the sales of this soap by ten in that period. This is what is meant by gathering specific materials.

「徹底了解產品和消費者」這句老生常談，真正的意涵便在於此。但，許多人還沒走到這一步就已經放棄。當兩樣東西表面上看起來沒什麼明顯的差異時，我們就認定兩者之間毫無差異存在。但只要探索得夠深、觀察得夠久，你幾乎一定會發現到，每一樣產品和某些消費者之間都存在了某種關係，而且這個關係是可以發展成創意的。

讓我舉個知名肥皂的廣告為例。也許你會說，市面上已經出現過那麼多肥皂廣告了，還有什麼新鮮的點子可以發揮？可是，有人針對肥皂和皮膚及頭髮之間的關連性做了研究，並針對該主題出版一本份量頗重的書，結果，這本書帶給廣告工作者許多靈感，令該肥皂的銷售量在五年內成長了十倍。這就是我所謂蒐集特定素材的意思。

Of equal importance with the gathering of these specific materials is the continuous process of gathering general materials.

Every really good creative person in advertising whom I have ever know has always had two noticeable characteristics. First, there was no subject under the sun in which he could not easily get interested— from, say, Egyptian burial customs to modern art. Every facet of life had fascination for him. Second, he was an extensive browser in all sorts of fields of information. For it is with the advertising man as with the cow: no browsing, no milk.

Now this gathering of general materials is important because this is where the previously stated principle comes in—namely, that an idea is nothing more nor less than a new combination of elements. In advertising an idea results from a new combination of **specific knowledge** about products and people with **general knowledge** about life and events.

除了蒐集特定素材，另一個同等重要的工作是，持續蒐集一般性的素材。

從以前到現在，我在廣告界碰到的每一位優秀的創意人才，都具備兩個顯著的特質。第一，他們對許多事都具備強烈的好奇心，從古埃及的葬儀到現代藝術，生活中的點點滴滴都是他們可以探索或挖掘的對象。第二，這些人會廣泛涉獵各個領域的資訊。廣告人就像乳牛，不吃草就分泌不出乳汁來。

蒐集一般性素材之所以重要，原因就在於前面提到過的那項原則：所謂創意，不過就是舊元素的重新組合。廣告上的創意，往往就是將產品和消費者的**特定資訊**，以及生活或時事的**一般性資訊**，加以重新組合的結果。

The process is something like that which takes place in the kaleidoscope. The kaleidoscope, as you know, is an instrument which designers sometimes use in searching for new patterns. It has little pieces of colored glass in it, and when these are viewed through a prism they reveal all sorts of geometrical designs. Every turn of its crank shifts these bits of glass into a new relationship and reveals a new pattern. The mathematical possibilities of such new combinations in the kaleidoscope are enormous, and the greater the number of pieces of glass in it the greater become the possibilities for new and striking combinations.

So it is with the production of ideas for advertising—or anything else. The construction of an advertisement is the construction of a new pattern in this kaleidoscopic world in which we live. The more of the elements of that world which are stored away in that pattern-making machine, the mind, the more the chances are increased for the production of new and striking combinations, or ideas. Advertising students who get restless about the "practical" value of general college subjects might consider this.

這個過程，和萬花筒的道理有點類似。我們知道，從事設計工作的人有時候會透過萬花筒來尋找新的花樣。萬花筒裡的有色玻璃碎片，透過三稜鏡的折射，會呈現出各式各樣的幾何圖案。每轉動一次萬花筒，這些玻璃碎片就會形成新的關係，呈現出不同的面貌。在數學上，這些玻璃碎片所能組合出的形態，可能性非常多，而且，萬花筒裡的玻璃碎片越多，它可能組合出的形態也就越多。

創意的生產也是同樣的道理──不論你談的是廣告創意還是其他方面的創意。因此，製作一支廣告，其實就是在我們這個如萬花筒般的世界建構出一個新型態、新花樣。我們的心智，是製造這些型態或花樣的機器，當這部機器裡儲存了越多關於這個世界的元素，它就越有機會創造出新鮮的、亮眼的組合和創意來。如果你正在學廣告，如果你懷疑學校要你修的那些非專業課程究竟有什麼「實用」價值，請你仔細想想這個道理。

This, then, is the first step in the technique of producing ideas: the gathering of materials. Part of it, you will see, is a current job and part of it is a life-long job. Before passing on to the next step there are two practical suggestions I might make about this material-gathering process.

The first is that if you have any sizable job of specific material gathering to do it is useful to learn the card-index method of doing it.

This is simply to get yourself a supply of those little 3 x 5 ruled white cards and use them to write down the items of specific information as you gather them. If you do this, one item to a card, after a while you can begin to classify them by sections of your subject. Eventually you will have a whole file box of them, neatly classified.

以上所說，便是創意生產的第一步驟：蒐集素材。有些素材，你只要蒐集一次就夠，有些卻是你一輩子都要關心的。在介紹下一個步驟之前，我想就蒐集素材這個過程給各位兩點實用的建議。

第一個建議是，如果你要蒐集的特定素材頗多，你最好學會卡片索引法。

這個方法很簡單，就是準備一些 3×5 吋、有畫線的白色索引卡，再將你蒐集到的特定資料寫在上面，一張卡片記錄一項資訊。一段時間之後，你便可以將這些資料分門別類，最後就會累積出一整箱分類清楚的索引卡。

The advantage of this method is not merely in such things as bringing order into your work and disclosing gaps in your knowledge. It lies even more in the fact that it keeps you from shirking the material-gathering job and by forcing your mind to go through the expression of your material in writing really prepares it to perform its idea-producing processes.

The second suggestion is that for storing up certain kinds of general material some method of doing it like a scrapbook or file is useful.

You will remember the famous scrapbooks which appear throughout the Sherlock Holmes stories and how the master detective spent his spare time indexing and cross-indexing the odd bits of material he gathered there. We run across an enormous amount of fugitive material which can be grist to the idea-producer's mill—newspaper clippings, publication articles, and original observations. Out of such material it is possible to build a useful source book of ideas.

這個方法的優點在於，它可以讓你的資料蒐集工作變得更井然有序，也可以顯示你的知識有哪些不足之處。更重要的是，這樣做可以對抗你的惰性，逼著你去蒐集資料，讓你的腦袋為創意生產的工作做準備。

其次，用剪貼簿或檔案夾來蒐集特定資料也是不錯的作法。

不曉得各位還記不記得？在福爾摩斯（Sherlock Holmes）的故事中，這位大偵探經常在空閒時將他蒐集到的零碎資料編製索引和交叉索引。我們在日常生活中碰到的許多資料，如剪報、刊物上的文章、第一手的觀察等等，都可能成為創意的原料。經過一段時間的累積，這些原料或許就會變成一本有用的靈感手冊。

Once I jotted in such a book the question: "Why does every man hope his first child will be a boy?" Five years later it became the headline and idea for one of the most successful advertisements I ever produced.

例如，我曾經在這樣的本子上寫下一個問題：「為什麼每個男人都希望自己的第一胎是男孩？」五年後，我從這個問題中得到靈感，做出了一則我有史以來最成功的廣告。

把蒐集到的資料當成食物，好好咀嚼一番，
等你的腦袋徹底消化吸收後，徹底放下，
讓潛意識為你工作

讓腦袋消化它

The Mental Digestive Process

The Mental Digestive Process

Now, assuming that you have done a workmanlike job of gathering material—that you have really worked at the first step—what is the next part of the process that the mind must go through? It is the process of masticating these materials, as you would food that you are preparing for digestion.

This part of the process is harder to describe in concrete terms because it goes on entirely inside your head.

What you do is to take the different bits of material which you have gathered and feel them all over, as it were, with the tentacles of the mind. You take one fact, turn it this way and that, look at it in different lights, and feel for the meaning of it. You bring two facts together and see how they fit.

讓腦袋消化它

假使你在第一步驟——資料蒐集——真的下了苦功，那麼接下來，你必須把這些資料當成食物，好好地咀嚼一番，你的腦袋才能夠消化吸收。

但由於這個過程完全發生在你的腦袋裡，因此較難用具體的文字加以描述。

總之，你要展開心智的觸鬚，完整地去感受你所蒐集的各種資料。你可以將某個事實放在不同的燈光下，用不同的角度去看它，並試圖摸索出它的意義。接著，將兩個不同的事實放在一起，看看它們之間有何關連。

What you are seeking now is the relationship, a synthesis where everything will come together in a neat combination, like a jig-saw puzzle.

And here a strange element comes in. This is that facts sometimes yield up their meaning quicker when you do not scan them too directly, too literally. You remember the winged messenger whose wings could only be seen when glanced at obliquely? It is like that. In fact, it is almost like listening for the meaning instead of looking for it. When creative people are in this stage of the process they get their reputation for absentmindedness.

As you go through this part of the process two things will happen. First, little tentative or partial ideas will come to you. Put these down on paper. Never mind how crazy or incomplete they seem: get them down. These are foreshadowings of the real idea that is to come, and expressing these in words forwards the process. Here again the little 3 x 5 cards are useful.

換言之，你要尋找的是不同事物之間的關係，像玩拼圖一樣將不同的資料整合起來。

這個過程會動用到一個奇特的元素。那就是，有時候，當我們用比較間接、迂迴的角度去看事情時，其意義反而更容易彰顯出來。還記得神話中那個長有翅膀的信差嗎？據說，若要看到他的翅膀，你不能正眼看他，而要斜眼瞥視才看得到。這個過程也是如此。我們甚至可以說，事物的意義是「聽」出來而不是「看」出來的。創意人在進行這個過程時，很容易被認為心不在焉。

過程中可能會發生兩件事。第一，你的腦袋中會出現一些不成熟、不完整的靈感。把這些靈感寫下來，不要管這些想法有多瘋狂或多不完整，寫下來就是了。這些小小的靈感，可能是真正創意的雛形。將這些想法試著用文字加以表達，可加速這個過程。這個時候，那些 3×5 吋的小卡片將再度發揮作用。

The second thing that will happen is that, by and by, you will get very tired of trying to fit your puzzle together. Let me beg of you not to get tired too soon. The mind, too, has a second wind. Go after at least this second layer of mental energy in this process. Keep trying to get one or more partial thoughts onto your little cards.

But after a while you will reach the hopeless stage. Everything is a jumble in your mind, with no clear insight anywhere. When you reach this point, if you have first really persisted in efforts to fit your puzzle together, then the second stage in the whole process is completed, and you are ready for the third one.

In this third stage you make absolutely no effort of a direct nature. You drop the whole subject and put the problem out of your mind as completely as you can.

第二件可能發生的事情是，你會越來越厭倦這項「拼圖」工作。但是，請別太快厭倦。人的腦袋，也是有所謂「再生氣」[1]（second wind）的。在這個過程中，請設法讓你的心智發揮其第二波的能量，將一個或更多不完整的靈感寫在你的小卡片上。

再過一陣子，你將來到全然無助的階段，你可能覺得自己腦袋打結，靈感完全枯竭。如果你先前有下工夫「拼圖」的話，那麼此時你便完成了第二階段，可以準備進入下一階段了。

在第三階段，你不需要做任何直接的努力，只要把整件事徹底放下，盡量不去想它就行。

---

1 編註：所謂再生氣，是指在長時間的運動之後，由運動初期所產生的苦惱或疲勞的感覺，經持續運動後突然轉變為舒暢感的一種變化。

It is important to realize that this is just as definite and just as necessary a stage in the process as the two preceding ones. What you have to do at this time, apparently, is to turn the problem over to your unconscious mind and let it work while you sleep.

There is one thing you can do in this stage which will help both to put the problem out of consciousness and to stimulate the unconscious, creative processes.

You remember how Sherlock Holmes used to stop right in the middle of a case and drag Watson off to a concert? That was a very irritating procedure to the practical and literalminded Watson. But Conan Doyle was a creator and knew the creative processes.

但各位要知道，這個階段和前面兩個階段比起來，是同樣明確而且必要的。只不過這次你所要做的，是把問題交給你的潛意識，讓它在你睡覺的時候為你工作。

儘管如此，你在這個階段還是有事可做，好幫你把問題從意識趕到潛意識，並刺激你的潛意識投入創造過程。

不曉得各位還記不記得，神探福爾摩斯常常在案件偵查到一半時，忽然拉著華生（Watson）一起去聽音樂會？這對個性務實、一板一眼的華生而言，實在是很討厭的事。但各位要知道，柯南・道爾[2]（Conan Doyle）是個道道地地的創意生產者，他對創意的生產過程清楚得很。

---

2 編註：柯南・道爾 (1859-1930) 出生於蘇格蘭愛丁堡，自幼即喜愛文學，14 歲便能閱讀英、法文學作品。1887 年，他的第一部偵探小說《血字的研究》出版，夏洛克・福爾摩斯和華生醫生正式出現在大眾眼前。 1890 年《四個簽名》的出版更是將福爾摩斯推向巔峰。1891 年，他正式棄醫從文，全力投入寫作，被譽為「世界偵探小說之父」。

So when you reach this third stage in the production of an idea, drop the problem completely and turn to whatever stimulates your imagination and emotions. Listen to music, go to the theater or movies, read poetry or a detective story.

In the first stage you have gathered your food. In the second you have masticated it well. Now the digestive process is on. Let it alone—but stimulate the flow of gastric juices.

因此，當你到達創意生產的第三階段，請徹底放下問題，改做一些其他的事，比方說聽音樂、看戲、看電影、讀詩、讀偵探小說。總之，只要能刺激你的想像或感受的都好。

在第一階段，你蒐集了很多食物。在第二階段，你將這些食物好好地咀嚼。如今，你的身體開始進行消化吸收了，你不用刻意理會，只要刺激你的身體分泌胃液就行。

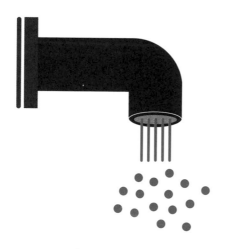

創意就是這麼來的：一開始念茲在茲，然後完全放下 ……
接著，創意就會突然湧現，彷彿無中生有一般

念茲在茲

"Constantly Thinking About It"

"Constantly Thinking About It"

Now, if you have really done your part in these three stages of the process you will almost surely experience the fourth.

Out of nowhere the Idea will appear.

It will come to you when you are least expecting it—while shaving, or bathing, or most often when you are half awake in the morning. It may waken you in the middle of the night.

Here, for instance, is the way it happens according to Mary Roberts Rinehart. In her story "Miss Pinkerton" she makes this character say:

念茲在茲

現在，假使你在前面三個階段都真正下過功夫，你一定會經歷第四階段。

那就是：創意會突然湧現，彷彿無中生有一般。

而且，它的出現，往往是在你最意想不到的時候。譬如，你可能正在刮鬍子，正在洗澡，或早上剛醒來，意識還迷迷糊糊的時候。此外，它也可能在三更半夜的時候把你吵醒。

譬如，推理小說家瑪麗・蘭哈特[1]（Mary Roberts Rinehart），曾經在她的作品〈平克頓小姐〉（*Miss Pinkerton*）中，透過某個角色談到創意出現的過程：

---

1 編註：瑪麗・蘭哈特 (1876-1958) 是一位多產作家，常被稱為「美國的阿嘉莎・克莉斯蒂（Agatha Christie，英國著名的女性推理小說家）」。在二〇年代，她是美國稿酬最豐的作家，隻手創造出一個推理小說的流派〔論者稱之為「早知如此」（Had I but known）流派〕。

And it was while I was folding up that copy of the Eagle and putting it away for later reading that something came into my mind. I have had this happen before; I can puzzle over a thing until I am in a state of utter confusion, give it up, and then suddenly have the answer leap into my mind without any apparent reason.

And here again is the way it happened in the discovery of the half-tone printing process, as told by Mr. Ives, the inventor of it:

While operating my photostereotype process in Ithaca I studied the problem of half-tone process [first step]. I went to bed one night in a state of brainfag over the problem [end of second and beginning of third step] and the instant that I woke in the morning [end of third step] saw before me, apparently projected on the ceiling, the completely worked-out process and equipment in operation [fourth step].

———那天，我正要把《老鷹》雜誌收起來，腦海中忽然出現一個靈感。這種狀況以前也發生過。我可能為了一個問題百思不得其解，最後困惑到了極點，只好放棄，結果，問題的答案卻在最意想不到的時候突然跳進我的腦海裡。

半色調印刷法（half-toneprintingprocess）的發明人伊維斯先生[2]（Mr. Ives），也曾經談到他發現該方法的過程：

———當我在綺色佳（Ithaca）進行過網照相製板（photostereotype process）時，我研究了半色調印刷法的問題〔步驟 1〕。某天晚上，我帶著滿腦的疑惑上床睡覺〔步驟 2 的結束和步驟 3 的開始〕。隔天早上醒來時，該印刷法的整個運作過程和機器的運作情形，卻浮現在我的腦海裡，而且如同投射在天花板上一樣清晰〔步驟 4〕。

---

2 編註：Frederick Eugene Ives，1856-1937。美國發明家和攝影家。

This is the way ideas come: after you have stopped straining for them and have passed through a period of rest and relaxation from the search.

Thus the story about Sir Isaac Newton and his discovery of the law of gravitation is probably not the whole truth. You will remember that when a lady asked the famous scientist how he came to make the discovery he is said to have replied, "By constantly thinking about it."

It was by constantly thinking about it that he made the discovery possible. But I suspect that if we knew the full history of the case we should find that the actual solution came while he was taking a walk in the country.

創意就是這麼來的：一開始你戮力以赴，接著你放下努力，讓自己放鬆和休息一段時間，接著，創意就出現了。

我們都聽過牛頓（Sir Issac Newton）是如何發現萬有引力定律的，但我們聽到的或許並非故事的全貌。曾經有一位名媛問這位鼎鼎大名的科學家說，他究竟是如何發現地心引力的？據說，牛頓當時的回答是：「靠著念茲在茲。」

沒錯，念茲在茲，應該是牛頓這項偉大發現的重要關鍵。但我猜想，要是我們知道整個過程，或許會發現，問題的答案，有可能是牛頓在鄉間散步時冒出來的。

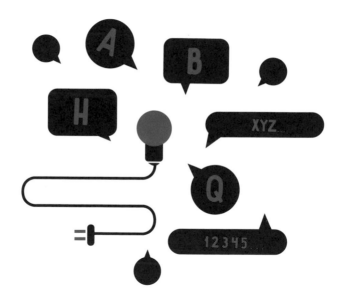

将你刚诞生的创意带到现实世界接受考验

最終階段

The Final Stage

The Final Stage

One more stage you have to pass through to complete the idea-producing process: the stage which might be called the cold, gray dawn of the morning after.

In this stage you have to take your little newborn idea out into the world of reality. And when you do you usually find that it is not quite the marvelous child it seemed when you first gave birth to it.

It requires a deal of patient working over to make most ideas fit the exact conditions, or the practical exigencies, under which they must work. And here is where many good ideas are lost. The idea man, like the inventor, is often not patient enough or practical enough to go through with this adapting part of the process. But it has to be done if you are to put ideas to work in a work-a-day world.

最終階段

還要經歷一個階段,整個創意生產過程才告完成。這個階段,或許可比喻為寒冷陰鬱的翌日清晨。

在本階段,你必須將你剛誕生的那個小小的創意,帶到現實世界以接受考驗。此時你通常會發現,這個美妙的新生兒並不如你原本想像得那麼完美。

大多數的創意要符合真實狀況和實務要求,都需要創意生產者有耐心地進行再加工。許多很好的創意,卻都是在這個階段化為幻影。許多創意工作者和發明家一樣,往往不夠有耐心或不夠務實,而無法走完這個調整和修正的階段。但如果你希望你的創意能夠真正在現實世界發揮作用,本階段的工作是一定要完成的。

Do not make the mistake of holding your idea close to your chest at this stage. Submit it to the criticism of the judicious.

When you do, a surprising thing will happen. You will find that a good idea has, as it were, self-expanding qualities. It stimulates those who see it to add to it. Thus possibilities in it which you have overlooked will come to light.

This, then, is the whole process or method by which ideas are produced:

First, the gathering of raw materials—both the materials of your immediate problem and the materials which come from a constant enrichment of your store of general knowledge.

請不要敝帚自珍，將你的創意拿給有眼光的人看，他們或許能提出建設性的批評。

一旦你這麼做，你將得到一個意外的收穫。你會發現，良好的創意具有自我擴充的特質。它會激發看得見它的人產生更多想法，讓它變得更加完備。結果，原本被你忽視的某些可能性，或許會因而開發出來。

以下，讓我將創意生產的整個過程或方法再總結一次：

首先，蒐集原始素材——包括與你的工作主題直接相關的素材，以及你平時累積的一般性素材。

Second, the working over of these materials in your mind.

Third, the incubating stage, where you let something beside the conscious mind do the work of synthesis.

Fourth, the actual birth of the Idea—the "Eureka! I have it!" stage.

And fifth, the final shaping and development of the idea to practical usefulness.

1 蒐集原始素材

第二，在腦海裡將這些素材加以咀嚼、消化和吸收。

第三，孵蛋階段：將問題交給你的潛意識進行統整。

第四，創意的誕生，也就是「啊！我找到了！」的階段。

最後，將你的創意做進一步的修正與發展，以符合實際用途。

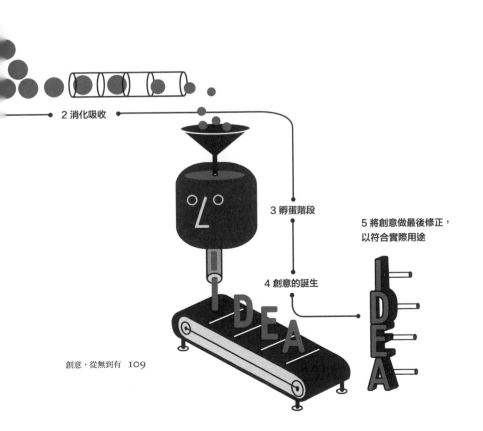

2 消化吸收

3 孵蛋階段

4 創意的誕生

5 將創意做最後修正，
以符合實際用途

創意人必備的原則：不斷拓展自己的人生經驗！

有些廣告（創意），沒有一定的人生經驗，是寫不出來的

幾點補充

Some After-Thoughts

Some After-Thoughts

Let me express my gratification at the number of letters which have come to me from readers of the earlier editions. The most gratifying have come from people who say "It works!"—that they have followed the prescription and gotten results.

Many have been from other creative people, entirely outside advertising—poets, painters, engineers, scientists, and even one writer of legal briefs—who say I have described their own experience. This supporting evidence will, I hope, encourage the beginner.

From my own further experience in advertising, government, and public affairs I find no essential points which I would modify in the idea-producing process. There is one, however, on which I would put greater emphasis. This is as to the store of **general** materials in the idea-producer's reservoir. I beg leave to illustrate this by a personal reference.

幾點補充

在本書出版後，我收到許多讀者的來函。有些人表示，他們按照書中介紹的步驟去做，得到了不錯的成效，令身為作者的我感到欣慰萬分。

這些讀者，有不少人並不是在廣告界工作的，其中包括詩人、畫家、工程師、科學家，甚至還有一位是專門寫辯護狀的。這些人告訴我，我在書中所描述的過程，和他們的親身經驗非常吻合。這些人的心聲，希望可以給剛入門的人多點信心。

此外，根據我自己在廣告界、政府機關和公共事務方面的經驗，我實在看不出這個創意生產過程有哪個重點是需要修正的。不過，其中有一點我倒是想多加強調。那就是，創意工作者平時就應該多多蒐集**一般性**素材，好豐富自己的資料庫。為了說明這一點，請容我花一點時間來談談我的親身經歷。

Some years ago I established my home in New Mexico and have been living there most of each year since. As a result I became interested in a whole new range of subjects, including Indian life, our Spanish history, native handicrafts, folkways of primitive people, etc.

Out of this grew some ideas about the possibilities of marketing some of the products of that region, by mail. I started with one of them—hand-woven neckties—wrote some advertisements about them, and copy-tested them. The result was a very tidy and interesting business.

The point is this: not only did the idea for starting the business come out of a general knowledge of the Southwest and its people, but all of the particular ideas for individual advertisements came from this source. If I had never gotten interested in Indian lore, Spanish-American history, the Spanish language, the handicraft philosophy, and so on, for their own sake, I would have had none of the reservoir of material which I believe made this advertising effective.

幾年前，我在新墨西哥州置產，此後的每一年，我大部分時間都在那裡度過。結果，我開始對很多東西產生興趣，例如：印地安人的生活、西班牙後裔的歷史、原住民的手工藝品和風俗習慣等等。

後來，我從中得到一個靈感：我或許可以透過郵購的方式銷售該地區的產品。一開始，我以手工領帶為試金石，寫了幾則廣告文案，再進行市場測試，結果創造了不俗的業績。

重點在於，我在這些年所累積、關於美國西南部及其民情風俗的一般性知識，不僅帶給我創業的靈感，也成為我在替該產品設計廣告時的創意泉源。要是我先前沒有對印地安民俗、西裔美國人的歷史、西班牙語、手工藝的哲學等主題產生興趣，就不可能累積出豐富的素材，讓我寫出打動人心的廣告來。

I have seen the truth of this principle a thousand times in practice. There are some advertisements you just cannot write until you have lived long enough—until, say, you have lived through certain experiences as a spouse, a parent, a businessman, or what not. The cycle of the years does something to fill your reservoir, unless you refuse to live spatially and emotionally.

But you can also enormously expand your experience, vicariously. It was the author of *Sard Harker*, I believe, who had never been to South America, yet wrote a corking good adventure book about it. I am convinced, however, that you gather this vicarious experience best, not when you are boning up on it for an immediate purpose, but when you are pursuing it as an end in itself.

我在實務上看過不下千次，這個原則確實是成立的。有些廣告，沒有一定的人生經驗就寫不出來，譬如，你可能要結過婚、有過小孩、做過生意，才知道什麼樣的廣告能夠打動有過類似經驗的人。歲月的累積，確實可以豐富你的資料庫，除非你劃地自限，不肯全心投入於生活當中。

不過，經驗也可以透過間接的方式大量累積。據我所知，《薩德‧哈克》[1]（*Sard Harker*）的作者雖然沒到過南美洲，卻寫出了一本精彩萬分的南美洲歷險記。不過，要充分吸收他人的經驗，你最好把它當做目的本身，而不是為了某個立即性的因素才臨時抱佛腳。

---

1 編註： 是一本由梅斯菲爾德（John Masefield，1878-1967，二十世紀英國桂冠詩人）所著的冒險小說，於 1924 年 10 月出版。

Of course, if you consider that your education was finished when you left college and wouldn't be caught dead with a copy of, say, one of Jane Austen's novels under your pillow, go no farther. In that case you will probably never know how the landed gentry of nineteenth century England scorned people "in trade," nor have any ideas about why the Hudson River Squire strain in this country does the same. And that just possibly, some day, might keep you from producing a really effective series of "snob appeal" advertisements for the"carriage trade." Of course, this is a disappearing race, so maybe it doesn't matter.

But the principle of constantly expanding your experience, both personally and vicariously, does matter tremendously in any idea-producing job. Make no mistake about that.

當然，要是你認為大學畢業就等於教育的終點，要是你不肯在枕頭下放一本珍・奧斯汀[2]（Jane Austen）的小說，那麼你應該不用再讀下去了。因為，你大概永遠不會知道，十九世紀的英國地主階級，是如何鄙視當時的生意人；你大概也不可能了解，美國哈德遜河畔的鄉紳們為何也抱持同樣的心態。因此，你日後應該無法創造出一則能夠訴諸上層階級勢利心態的廣告。當然，由於這類人已經瀕臨絕種，這對你來說或許無關緊要。

總之，不斷拓展自己的人生經驗（包括自己的親身體驗和透過他人所得到的間接經驗）這個原則，對任何創意生產工作而言都非常重要。請切記這個道理。

---

2 編註：珍・奧斯汀 (1775-1817) 為英國著名小說家，作品有《傲慢與偏見》、《理性與感性》、《曼斯菲爾莊園》、《愛瑪》等，並被公認為英國文學中作品流傳最廣、最受人喜受的作家。

Another point to encourage you. No doubt you have seen people who seem to spark ideas—good ideas—right off the "top of their heads," without ever going through all this process which I have described.

Sometimes you have only seen the "Eureka! I have it!" stage take place. But sometimes you have also seen the fruits of long discipline in the practices here advocated. This discipline produces a mind so well stocked, and so quick at discerning relationships, as to be capable of such fast production.

Still another point I might elaborate on a little is about words. We tend to forget that words are, themselves, ideas. They might be called ideas in a state of suspended animation. When the words are mastered the ideas tend to come alive again.

然而，相信各位一定都看過，有些人好像擁有源源不絕的創意，似乎不需要經過我剛剛描述的那整個過程，就能夠不假思索地丟出一個靈感來。

但我要提醒各位，有些時候，我們只看到「啊！我找到了！」這個階段，卻忽略了一個事實：很多創意，其實是長期從事心智鍛鍊的成果。有些人經過長時期的鍛鍊，腦袋裡累積了許多素材，能敏銳地覺察到事物間的關連性，因此能很快地拋出創意來。

還有一項重點是我想再多加著墨的，那就是文字。我們很容易忘記，文字本身就是概念，又或者，是處於生命暫停（suspended animation）狀態的概念。一旦掌握了文字，相關的概念往往會再度「復活」。

Take the word *semantics*, for example. The chances are you will never use it in an advertisement. But if you have it in your vocabulary you will have a number of ideas about the use of words as symbols which will be of very practical value indeed. (If you don't have it in your vocabulary, look up Hayakawa's *Language in Thought and Action.*)

Thus, words being symbols of ideas, we can collect ideas by collecting words. The fellow who said he tried reading the dictionary but couldn't get the hang of the story simply missed the point: namely, that it is a collection of short stories.

以「語意學」一詞為例。這個詞出現在廣告中的機會，應該微乎其微。但如果你的詞彙中有這個詞的存在，你應該或多或少了解文字是象徵的道理，而這，是非常具實用價值的。（要是你還不懂這個詞的意思，請查閱早川博士的《語言與人生》[3]。）

既然文字是概念的象徵，我們就可以透過蒐集字詞來蒐集概念。要是有人說，他在讀過字典之後掌握不到它主要的故事情節，那他就誤解了字典的用意──字典是許多短篇故事的集合。

---

[3] 編註： S. I. Hayakawa，1906-1992。美國心理學家、語意學權威、老師及作家，曾擔任美國參議員。 *Language in Thought and Action*，中譯本由遠流出版。

And, finally, let me suggest a few other books which will expand your understanding of this whole idea-producing process:

· *The Art of Thought* by Graham Wallas. Published by Jonathan Cape, Ltd., London.

· *Science and Method* by H. Poincaré. Translation by F. Maitland. Published by Thos. Nelson & Sons, London.

· *The Art of Scientific Investigation* by W. I. B. Beveridge. A Modern Library paperback edition.

最後，為幫助各位更徹底了解整個創意生產的過程，我要推薦以下三本書：

- 《思考的方法》(*The Art of Thought*)，作者華勒士（Graham Wallas）[4]

- 《科學與方法》(*Science and Method*)，作者龐加萊（H. Poincaré）[5]

- 《科學之路》(*The Art of Scientific Investigation*)，作者貝弗里奇（W. I. B. Beveridge）[6]

---

4 編註： Graham Wallas，1858-1932。英國社會學家及心理學家。 *The Art of Thought*，中譯本由台灣商務出版。

5 編註： Henri Poincaré，1854-1912。法國數學家和物理學家，也是科學界的哲人。

6 譯註： *The Art of Scientific Investigation* ，中譯本由長堤出版。

大師小傳
About The Author

他，12 歲就踏入社會。

他，26 歲進入智威湯遜廣告公司（JWT）。

他，33 歲主導全美第一個公開談論「體味」的體香劑廣告，爭議性與話題性十足，

並創下銷售佳績。

他，44 歲成為芝加哥大學專任教授。

他，著作不多，但本本經典。

他，60 歲獲廣告界兩項殊榮的肯定—「年度廣告人獎」和「廣告獎金牌」。

他，78 歲從 JWT 退休後，到美國新墨西哥州種蘋果。

他，辭世一年後入選美國廣告名人堂。

他的一生充滿傳奇⋯⋯

他的影響力，直到今日仍深深影響著全球各界創意人；

他，就是美國廣告界永遠的大師——楊傑美（James Webb Young）。

楊傑美是美國著名廣告大師，亦是廣告創意魔島理論的集大成者。一九一二年，他進入智威湯遜廣告公司（JWT）工作，任職達52年之久，最初是從廣告文案做起，寫出了許多膾炙人口的經典文案，最後順利晉升為副總裁，成功將 JWT 推向全世界。

楊傑美的廣告生涯長達61年，幾乎可以與美國廣告發展史劃上等號。自一九三一年起，他於芝加哥大學商學院教授商業史和廣告學，本書的原型即為楊傑美在課堂上使用的講義。一九四六年，他獲頒「年度廣告人獎」（Advertising Man of the Year Award）和「廣告獎金牌」（Advertising Awards Gold Medal），以表彰他一直以來的卓越成就和二戰期間的卓越貢獻。一九七四年，即在他逝世一年後，獲全美廣告聯盟（American Advertising Federation）頒贈美國廣告界最高榮譽——「廣告殿堂榮譽獎」（Advertising Hall of Fame）。

國家圖書館出版品預行編目（CIP）資料

創意，從無到有 / 楊傑美 (James Webb Young)著；許晉福譯. -- 二版.
-- 臺北市：經濟新潮社出版：家庭傳媒城邦分公司發行, 2015.02
　　面；　公分. --（經營管理；121）

譯自：A technique for producing ideas

ISBN 978-986-6031-65-6(平裝)

1.創造性思考

176.4　　　　　　　　　　　　　　　　104001432